COOKING CLASS

P·A·S·T·A

COOKBOOK

PUBLICATIONS INTERNATIONAL, LTD.

PYREX is a registered trademark of Corning Incorporated, Corning, NY 14831.

ISBN: 0-7853-0192-5

Photography: Sacco Productions Limited, Chicago.

Pictured on the front cover: Fusilli Pizzaiolo *(page 46)*.
Pictured on the inside front cover: Angel Hair Pasta with Red Chili Sauce *(page 33)*.
Pictured on the back cover: Spinach Stuffed Manicotti *(page 74)*.

The publishers would like to thank the following companies and organizations for the use of their recipes in this publication: American Egg Board, A-OK Cook Off, Black-Eyed Pea Jamboree—Athens, Texas, Castroville Artichoke Festival, The Fresh Garlic Association, Kansas Poultry Association, Kansas State Board of Agriculture, National Pasta Association, New Jersey Department of Agriculture, North Dakota Beef Commission, North Dakota Cattlewomen, North Dakota Dairy Promotion Commission, North Dakota Wheat Commission, Pace Foods, Inc., Southeast United Dairy Industry Association, Inc. and Wisconsin Milk Marketing Board.

8 7 6 5 4 3 2 1

Manufactured in the U.S.A.

CONTENTS

Chicken Salad Deluxe (*page 10*)

Scallops with Vermicelli (*page 38*)

Sunday Supper Stuffed Shells (*page 62*)

CLASS NOTES

The recipes in *Cooking Class Pasta* show you how to make satisfying, delicious dishes out of versatile, economical and nutritious pasta. While there are over 150 varieties of pasta, we have featured the most popular shapes, such as fettuccine, shells, linguine and lasagna noodles. With step-by-step directions and helpful how-to photographs, you will discover how pasta makes a great addition to soups, salads, casseroles and skillet dishes. Pasta also makes a fantastic main course when topped with savory sauce or used as the base for ever-popular lasagna.

COOKING PASTA

Dry Pasta: For every pound of dry pasta, bring 4 to 6 quarts of water to a full, rolling boil. Add 2 teaspoons salt, if desired. Gradually add pasta, allowing water to return to a boil. The water helps circulate the pasta so that it cooks evenly. Stir frequently to prevent the pasta from sticking. Begin testing for doneness at the minimum recommended time given on the package directions. Pasta should be "al dente"—tender, yet firm, not mushy. Immediately drain pasta to prevent overcooking. For best results, toss the pasta with sauce immediately after draining. If the sauce is not ready, toss the pasta with some butter or oil to prevent it from sticking. Store dry uncooked pasta in a cool dry place.

Fresh Pasta: Homemade pasta takes less time to cook than dry pasta. Cook fresh pasta in the same manner as dry, except begin testing for doneness after 2 minutes. Fresh pasta will last several weeks in the refrigerator or it can be frozen for up to 1 month. Two basic fresh pasta preparation techniques, by hand and by machine, are explained in the recipe section.

EQUIPMENT

Pasta Machine: Pasta machines with hand-turned rollers are very useful in kneading and rolling pasta dough. Cutting attachments (fettuccine and angel hair are usually included) help to cut pasta evenly. Electric machines also mix the dough, however the pasta usually lacks the resilience of hand-worked dough and the machines are more expensive.

Paring Knife: A sharp knife with a thin 3- to 4-inch-long blade used for peeling and slicing fruits and vegetables and cutting or chopping herbs.

Utility Knife: A sharp knife with a thin 6- to 8-inch-long blade. It is used for the same purposes as a paring knife, but the longer blade can provide better leverage.

Chef's Knife: A sharp knife with a wide 6- to 10-inch-long blade. It is used for chopping and slicing large, thick items.

TIME-SAVING TIPS

• Plan on preparing an extra batch of your favorite pasta soup or sauce. Pour into serving-size freezer containers and freeze. Thaw and reheat for a last-minute dinner or quick lunch.

• Lasagna, manicotti and stuffed shells are perfect dishes to prepare and freeze for another time. Try freezing casseroles in single-serving portions for days when quick meals are necessary. Heat to serving temperature in the microwave or conventional oven.

• When cooking pasta, add extra to the boiling water so that you will have leftovers. If you like, toss the leftover pasta with a little olive oil to help prevent sticking. Use plain leftover pasta as a base or extender for salads, soups, side dishes and casseroles. Simply store the leftover pasta in a plastic bag in the refrigerator for up to 3 days. Freshen the pasta by rinsing with hot or cold water, depending on how you plan to use it. Pasta can also be frozen and then reheated in boiling water or microwaved for a fresh-cooked texture and taste.

• Combine leftover cooked meats, poultry, fish and vegetables with your favorite pasta shape and a simple sauce for a fast new meal.

• One cup of uncooked macaroni-type pasta will yield 2 cups cooked pasta.

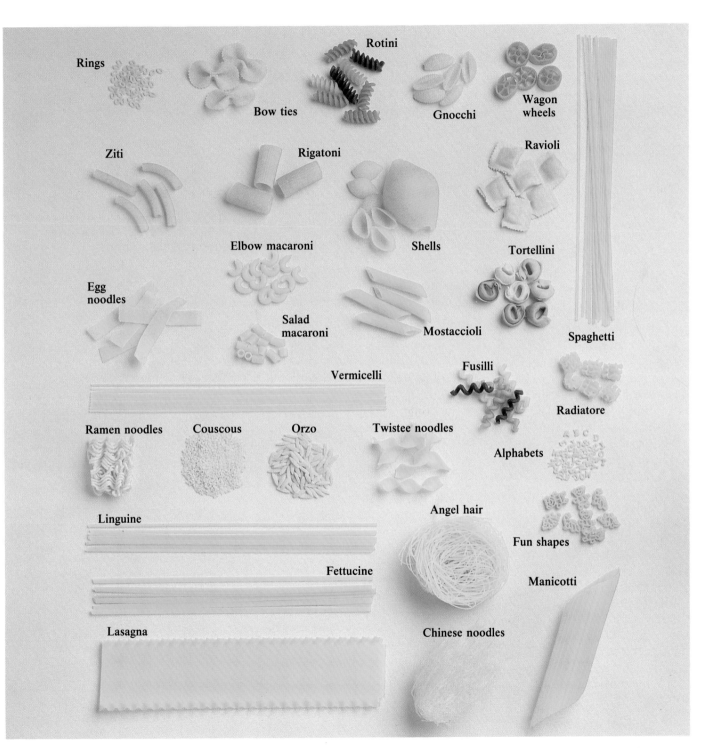

Rings

Rotini

Bow ties

Gnocchi

Wagon wheels

Ziti

Rigatoni

Ravioli

Elbow macaroni

Shells

Tortellini

Egg noodles

Salad macaroni

Mostaccioli

Spaghetti

Vermicelli

Fusilli

Radiatore

Ramen noodles

Couscous

Orzo

Twistee noodles

Alphabets

Linguine

Angel hair

Fun shapes

Fettucine

Manicotti

Lasagna

Chinese noodles

Thai Chicken Fettuccine Salad

3 boneless skinless chicken breast halves (about 15 ounces)
6 ounces fettuccine
1 cup PACE® Picante Sauce
¼ cup chunky peanut butter
2 tablespoons honey
2 tablespoons orange juice
1 teaspoon soy sauce
½ teaspoon ground ginger
2 tablespoons vegetable oil
Lettuce or savoy cabbage leaves (optional)
¼ cup coarsely chopped cilantro (see parsley, page 38)
¼ cup peanut halves
¼ cup thin red pepper strips, cut into halves
Additional PACE® Picante Sauce (optional)

1. Cut chicken into 1-inch pieces; set aside.

2. Cook pasta according to package directions. Drain in colander.

3. While pasta is cooking, combine 1 cup picante sauce, peanut butter, honey, orange juice, soy sauce and ginger in small saucepan. Cook and stir over low heat until blended and smooth. Reserve ¼ cup picante sauce mixture.

4. Place pasta in large bowl. Pour remaining picante sauce mixture over pasta; toss gently to coat.

5. Heat oil in large skillet over medium-high heat until hot. Cook and stir chicken in hot oil about 5 minutes until chicken is browned on the outside and no longer pink in center.

6. Add reserved picante sauce mixture; mix well.

7. Arrange pasta on lettuce-lined platter. Place chicken mixture on pasta. Top with cilantro, peanut halves and pepper strips.

8. Refrigerate until mixture is cooled to room temperature. Serve with additional picante sauce. Garnish, if desired.

Makes 4 servings

Step 1. Cutting chicken breast halves into 1-inch pieces.

Step 3. Cooking and stirring sauce.

Step 5. Cutting into chicken to test doneness.

Chicken Salad Deluxe

1 1/4 cups prepared buttermilk salad
    dressing
1/2 cup mayonnaise
3 tablespoons half-and-half
1 3/4 teaspoons Beau Monde
    seasoning
1 teaspoon salt
1/2 teaspoon pepper
1 1/2 pounds boneless skinless
    chicken breast halves
1 small onion, cut into slices
1 rib celery, chopped
1 carrot, coarsely chopped
10 ounces 100% semolina medium
    shell macaroni
3 cups diced celery
2 1/2 cups seedless green grapes, cut
    lengthwise into halves
1 package (12 ounces) slivered
    almonds (reserve 1 tablespoon
    for garnish)
2 cans (2 1/4 ounces each) sliced
    water chestnuts, drained
1 medium onion, chopped
    (page 26)
    Lettuce leaves (optional)
    Parsley and sliced star fruit for
    garnish
    Cantaloupe slices

1. Combine salad dressing, mayonnaise, half-and-half, seasoning, salt and pepper in small bowl until well blended. Cover; refrigerate overnight to blend flavors.

2. Place chicken, onion slices, chopped celery and carrot in Dutch oven. Add enough cold water to cover. Cover and bring to a boil over medium heat. Reduce heat to low. Simmer 5 to 7 minutes until chicken is no longer pink in center.

3. Drain chicken, discarding vegetables and liquid. Refrigerate chicken until it is cool enough to handle. Cut chicken into 1/2-inch pieces. Set aside.

4. Cook shells according to package directions. Drain well, then cover and refrigerate until chilled.

5. Combine chicken, shells, diced celery, grapes, almonds, water chestnuts and chopped onion in large bowl. Pour dressing over salad; toss gently to coat. Serve on lettuce-lined plates. Garnish, if desired. Serve with cantaloupe slices. *Makes 20 servings*

Step 2. Adding water to Dutch oven to cover chicken mixture.

Step 3. Cutting chicken into 1/2-inch pieces.

Rainbow Pasta Salad

8 ounces tricolor corkscrew pasta
½ pound medium raw shrimp *or*
  2 cans (4½ ounces each)
  medium shrimp, drained
½ cup chopped walnuts (optional)
¼ cup French salad dressing
¼ cup mayonnaise
2 tablespoons sliced pimiento-
  stuffed green olives
1 teaspoon finely chopped onion
  Lettuce leaves
  Grape clusters and lemon peel
  strips for garnish

1. Cook pasta according to package directions. Drain in colander. Cover and refrigerate until chilled.

2. If using raw shrimp, they must be peeled and cooked. To peel shrimp, remove the legs by gently pulling them off the shell. Loosen shell with fingers, then slide off.

3. To devein shrimp, cut a shallow slit along back of shrimp with paring knife. Lift out intestinal vein. (You may find this easier to do under cold running water.) If desired, this step may be omitted.

4. To cook raw shrimp, place 2 cups salted water in 2-quart saucepan. Bring to a boil over high heat. Add shrimp; reduce heat to low. Simmer 3 to 5 minutes until shrimp turn pink and opaque. Remove from heat; drain well. Refrigerate shrimp until thoroughly chilled.

5. Combine pasta, shrimp, walnuts, salad dressing, mayonnaise, olives and onion in large bowl; toss gently to coat.

6. Cover; refrigerate at least 2 hours. Serve over lettuce. Garnish, if desired.

Makes 4 servings

Step 2. Removing shells from shrimp.

Step 3. Deveining shrimp.

Step 5. Tossing salad to coat with dressing.

Seafood Pea-Ista Salad

8 ounces corkscrew pasta
1 bunch broccoli
½ cup mayonnaise or salad
   dressing
¼ cup zesty Italian salad dressing
2 tablespoons grated Parmesan
   cheese
2 cups canned green or yellow
   black-eyed peas, rinsed
1½ cups chopped imitation
   crabmeat (about 8 ounces)
½ cup chopped green pepper
   (page 46)
½ cup chopped tomato (page 42)
¼ cup sliced green onions

1. Cook pasta according to package directions. Drain in colander.

2. Trim leaves from broccoli. Remove stalks. Cut broccoli into flowerets by removing each head to include a small piece of the stem. Cut enough flowerets to make 1 cup.

3. To partially cook broccoli, heat 1 quart lightly salted water in 2-quart saucepan over high heat to a boil. Add 1 cup broccoli flowerets. Return to a boil; boil 3 minutes until crisp-tender. Drain broccoli from saucepan, then immediately plunge into cold water to stop cooking. Drain and cool.

4. Combine mayonnaise, Italian salad dressing and cheese in large bowl until well blended.

5. Add pasta, broccoli, peas, imitation crabmeat, pepper, tomato and onions; toss gently to coat.

6. Cover; refrigerate at least 2 hours before serving. *Makes 4 to 6 servings*

Step 2. Cutting broccoli into flowerets.

Step 3. Plunging broccoli into cold water to stop cooking.

Step 4. Adding cheese to mayonnaise and dressing.

Fresh Seafood and Linguine Salad

1½ to 3 dozen clams
   Salt
  4 pounds mussels
1½ pounds small squid
  8 ounces linguine
   Olive oil
¼ cup freshly squeezed lemon
   juice
  2 cloves garlic, minced (page 26)
¼ teaspoon pepper
  1 red onion, thinly sliced and
   separated into rings for
   garnish
⅓ cup finely chopped Italian
   parsley for garnish (page 38)

1. Discard any clams that remain open when tapped with fingers. To clean clams, scrub with stiff brush under cold running water. Soak clams in mixture of ⅓ cup salt to 1 gallon of water for 20 minutes. Drain water; repeat two more times.

2. Discard any mussels that remain opened when tapped with fingers. To clean mussels, scrub with stiff brush under cold running water. To debeard, pull threads from shells with fingers. Soak mussels in mixture of ⅓ cup salt to 1 gallon of water for 20 minutes. Drain water; repeat two more times.

3. To clean each squid, hold body of squid firmly in one hand. Grasp head firmly with other hand; pull head, twisting gently from side to side. (Head and contents of body should pull away in one piece.) Set aside tubular body sac. Cut tentacles off head; set aside. Discard head and contents of body.

4. Grasp tip of pointed, thin, clear cartilage protruding from body; pull out and discard. Rinse squid under cold running water. Peel off and discard spotted outer membrane covering body sac and fins. Pull off side fins; set aside. Rinse inside of squid thoroughly under running water. Repeat with remaining squid.

continued on page 18

Step 2. Removing beards from mussels.

Step 3. Removing head from squid.

Step 4. Peeling outer membrane from squid.

**Fresh Seafood and Linguine Salad,
continued**

5. Cut crosswise into ¼-inch rings; finely chop tentacles and fins. (Rings, fins and reserved tentacles are all edible parts.) Pat pieces dry with paper towels.

6. To steam clams and mussels, place 1 cup water in large stockpot. Bring to a boil over high heat. Add clams and mussels. Cover stockpot; reduce heat to low. Steam 5 to 7 minutes until clams and mussels are opened. Remove from stockpot with slotted spoon. Discard any clams or mussels that remain closed.

7. Meanwhile, cook pasta according to package directions. Drain in colander. Place in large bowl and toss with 2 tablespoons olive oil.

8. Add just enough olive oil to large skillet to cover bottom. Heat over medium heat; add squid. Cook and stir 2 minutes until squid is opaque. Place squid in large glass bowl. Add pasta, mussels and clams.

9. Combine ½ cup olive oil, lemon juice, garlic, ½ teaspoon salt and pepper in small bowl; blend well. Pour over salad; toss gently to coat.

10. Cover; refrigerate at least 3 hours. Season with additional lemon juice, salt and pepper, if necessary. Garnish, if desired.   *Makes 6 servings*

Step 5. Cutting squid into rings.

Step 8. Removing cooked squid from skillet.

Pasta Salad in Artichoke Cups

5 cloves garlic, peeled (page 32)
½ cup white wine
6 medium artichokes for cups
1 lemon, cut into halves
6 cups chicken broth
1 tablespoon *plus* 1 teaspoon
  olive oil, divided
1 package (2 ounces) artichoke
  hearts
8 ounces corkscrew pasta or
  pasta twists
½ teaspoon dried basil leaves,
  crushed
  Basil Vinaigrette Dressing
  (page 20)

1. Place garlic and wine in 1-quart saucepan. Bring to a boil over high heat; reduce heat to low. Simmer 10 minutes.

2. Meanwhile, prepare artichokes. Cut bottoms from artichokes with utility knife so that artichokes will sit flat. Remove outer leaves.

3. Cut 1 inch off tops of artichokes. Snip tips from remaining leaves with scissors. To help prevent discoloration, rub ends with lemon.

4. Place chicken broth in 6-quart Dutch oven. Bring to a boil over high heat. Add artichokes, wine mixture and 1 tablespoon oil. Reduce heat to low. Cover; simmer 25 to 30 minutes or until leaves pull easily from base. Drain.

5. Cook artichoke hearts according to package directions. Drain well. Cut into slices to make 2 cups. Set aside.

continued on page 20

Step 2. Cutting off bottom of artichoke.

Step 3. Snipping tips from artichoke leaves.

Step 4. Testing doneness of artichokes.

***Pasta Salad in Artichoke Cups,
continued***

6. Cook pasta according to package directions. Drain in colander. Place pasta in large bowl. Sprinkle with remaining 1 teaspoon oil and basil.

7. Prepare Basil Vinaigrette Dressing.

8. Add artichoke hearts and 1 cup dressing to pasta; toss gently to coat.

9. Carefully spread outer leaves of whole artichokes. Remove small heart leaves by grasping with fingers, then pulling and twisting. Scoop out fuzzy choke with spoon.

10. Fill with pasta mixture. Cover; refrigerate until serving time. Serve with remaining dressing. Garnish as desired.

Makes 6 servings

Basil Vinaigrette Dressing

$^1/_3$ **cup white wine vinegar**
  2 tablespoons Dijon-style mustard
  3 cloves garlic, peeled (page 32)
$^3/_4$ **cup coarsely chopped fresh basil
    leaves**
  1 cup olive oil
    Salt and pepper to taste

1. Place vinegar, mustard and garlic in blender or food processor. Cover; process using an on/off pulsing action until garlic is well mixed. Add basil; continue to pulse until mixture is blended.

2. With motor running, slowly pour in olive oil. Season to taste with salt and pepper.

Makes about 1$^1/_2$ cups

Step 9. Scooping out choke from artichoke with spoon.

Step 10. Filling artichoke with pasta mixture.

Basil Vinaigrette Dressing: Step 2. Slowly pouring oil into food processor.

Rotini Salad

10 ounces rotini
2 to 3 stalks broccoli
1 can (6 ounces) small pitted ripe olives, drained
10 to 12 cherry tomatoes, cut into halves
½ medium red onion, cut into slivers
½ cup Italian salad dressing
1 to 2 tablespoons grated Parmesan cheese (optional)
Freshly ground black pepper
Carrot strips for garnish

1. Cook pasta according to package directions. Drain in colander. Cover and refrigerate until chilled.

2. Trim leaves from broccoli stalks. Trim ends of stalks. Cut broccoli into flowerets by removing each head to include a small piece of the stem. Peel stalks, then cut into 1-inch pieces.

3. To cook broccoli, heat 1 quart lightly salted water in 2-quart saucepan over high heat to a boil. Immediately add broccoli; return to a boil. Continue boiling, uncovered, 3 to 5 minutes until bright green and tender. Drain broccoli; rinse under cold water and drain thoroughly.

4. Combine pasta, broccoli, olives, tomatoes, onion and salad dressing in large bowl. Add cheese. Season to taste with pepper. Toss gently to coat.

5. Cover; refrigerate at least 2 hours. Garnish, if desired. *Makes 8 to 10 servings*

Step 2. Cutting broccoli stalk into 1-inch pieces.

Step 3. Rinsing cooked broccoli.

Step 4. Adding cheese to pasta mixture.

Shaker Chicken and Noodle Soup

13 cups chicken broth, divided
¼ cup dry vermouth
¼ cup butter or margarine
1 cup heavy cream
1 package (12 ounces) egg
**   noodles**
1 cup thinly sliced celery
1½ cups water
¾ cup all-purpose flour
2 cups diced cooked chicken*
**   Salt and pepper to taste**
¼ cup finely chopped parsley
**   (optional) (page 38)**

*To poach, then dice boneless skinless raw chicken breast halves, see page 10, steps 2 and 3.

1. Combine 1 cup broth, vermouth and butter in small saucepan. Bring to a boil over high heat. Continue to boil 15 to 20 minutes or until liquid is reduced to ¼ cup and has a syrupy consistency. Stir in cream. Set aside.

2. Bring remaining broth to a boil in Dutch oven. Add noodles and celery; cook until noodles are just tender.

3. Combine water and flour in medium bowl until smooth. Stir into broth mixture. Boil 2 minutes, stirring constantly.

4. Stir in reserved cream mixture; add chicken. Season with salt and pepper. Heat just to serving temperature. Do not boil. Sprinkle with parsley. Garnish as desired.

Makes 15 servings

Note: This soup freezes well.

Step 2. Adding celery to boiling broth.

Step 3. Stirring flour mixture into broth.

Quick Beef Soup

1 large onion
2 cloves garlic
1½ pounds lean ground beef
1 can (28 ounces) whole peeled
    tomatoes, undrained
6 cups water
6 beef bouillon cubes
¼ teaspoon pepper
½ cup uncooked orzo
1½ cups frozen peas, carrots and
    corn vegetable blend
    French bread (optional)

1. To chop onion, peel skin. Cut onion in half through the root. Place cut side down on cutting board. Holding knife horizontally, make cuts parallel to board almost to root end. Cut onion vertically into thin slices, holding onion with fingers to keep its shape. Turn onion and cut crosswise to root end. (The closer the cuts are spaced, the finer the onion is chopped.) Repeat with remaining onion half.

2. To mince garlic, trim ends of garlic cloves. Slightly crush clove under flat side of chef's knife blade; peel away skin. Chop garlic with chef's knife until garlic is in uniform fine pieces. Set aside.

3. Cook beef, onion and garlic in large saucepan over medium-high heat until beef is brown, stirring to separate meat; drain drippings.

4. Place tomatoes with juice in covered blender or food processor. Process until smooth.

5. Add tomatoes, water, bouillon cubes and pepper to meat mixture. Bring to a boil over high heat. Reduce heat to low. Simmer, uncovered, 20 minutes.

6. Add orzo and vegetables. Simmer 15 minutes more. Serve with French bread.

Makes 6 servings

Step 1. Chopping onion.

Step 2. Crushing garlic to remove skin.

Step 5. Stirring meat mixture.

Zucchini-Tomato-Noodle Soup

3 **pounds zucchini**
³/₄ **cup water**
¹/₂ **cup butter**
4 **cups chopped onions**
8 **cups tomatoes, cut into eighths**
1 **can (48 ounces) chicken broth**
3 **cloves garlic, chopped**
1 **teaspoon Beau Monde**
   seasoning
1 **teaspoon salt**
1 **teaspoon pepper**
1 **pound 100% durum noodles**
   Garlic bread (optional)

1. Scrub zucchini with vegetable brush under cold running water. Slice lengthwise into halves with utility knife. (If zucchini is large, cut into 4 lengthwise pieces.) Cut each half into 4 to 6 lengthwise strips. Holding strips together with fingers, cut crosswise into bite-size pieces.

2. Combine zucchini and water in stockpot; cover. Cook over medium-high heat 10 minutes until partially done, stirring twice.

3. Heat butter in large skillet over medium heat. Add onions; cook and stir in hot butter until tender.

4. Add onion mixture, tomatoes, broth, garlic, seasoning, salt and pepper to zucchini mixture; cover. Simmer 20 to 25 minutes.

5. Meanwhile, cook noodles according to package directions. Drain well.

6. Add noodles to soup; heat through. Serve with garlic bread.   *Makes 8 servings*

Step 1. Cutting zucchini into bite-size pieces.

Step 2. Adding water to stockpot.

Step 6. Adding noodles to soup.

Spinach-Garlic Pasta with Garlic-Onion Sauce

½ pound fresh spinach
6 eggs, divided
1½ cups all-purpose flour, divided
1 tablespoon olive oil
6 large cloves fresh garlic, minced (page 26)
½ teaspoon salt
Garlic-Onion Sauce (page 32)
Grated Parmesan cheese (optional)

1. Separate spinach into leaves. Swish in cold water. Repeat several times with fresh cold water to remove sand and grit. Pat dry with paper towels.

2. To remove stems from spinach leaves, fold each leaf in half, then with hand pull stem toward top of leaf. Discard stem.

3. To blanch spinach, heat 1 quart of lightly salted water in 2-quart saucepan over high heat to a boil. Immediately add spinach. Return to a boil; boil 2 to 3 minutes until crisp-tender. Drain spinach from saucepan, then immediately plunge into cold water to stop cooking. Place in colander to drain. Let stand until cool enough to handle. Squeeze spinach between hands to remove excess moisture. Finely chop with chef's knife.

4. To separate egg yolks from whites, gently tap egg in center against a hard surface, such as the side of a bowl. Holding a shell half in each hand, transfer yolk back and forth between shell halves. Allow the white to drip down between the 2 halves into a bowl.

5. When all the white has dripped into the bowl, place the yolk in another bowl. Place white in a third bowl. Repeat with 3 more eggs. Store unused egg whites in an airtight container. Refrigerate for about 1 week.

6. Place 1 cup flour on cutting board. Make well in center. Whisk 2 whole eggs, yolks and olive oil in small bowl until well blended. Gradually pour into well in flour mixture while mixing with fingertips or fork to form ball of dough.

Step 1. Washing spinach.

Step 2. Removing stems from spinach.

Step 4. Separating egg yolk from the white.

continued on page 32

Spinach-Garlic Pasta with Garlic-Onion Sauce, continued

7. Add spinach, garlic and salt. Mix, working in more flour as needed.

8. Place dough on lightly floured surface; flatten slightly. To knead dough, fold dough in half toward you and press dough away from you with heels of hands. Give dough a quarter turn and continue folding, pushing and turning. Continue kneading 5 minutes or until smooth and elastic, adding more flour to prevent sticking if necessary. Cover with plastic wrap. Let dough stand 15 minutes.

9. Unwrap dough and knead briefly as described in step 8 on lightly floured surface. Roll out dough to ⅛-inch-thick circle using lightly floured rolling pin. Gently pick up dough circle with both hands. Hold it up to the light to check for places where dough is too thick. Return to board; even out any thick spots. Let rest until dough is slightly dry but can be handled without breaking.

10. Lightly flour dough circle; roll loosely on to rolling pin. Slide rolling pin out; press dough roll gently with hand and cut into ¼-inch-wide strips with sharp knife. Carefully unfold strips.*

11. Prepare Garlic-Onion Sauce.

12. Cook pasta in large pot of boiling salted water 1 to 2 minutes just until tender. Drain in colander; pour into large bowl.

13. Toss sauce over pasta. Serve with cheese. Garnish as desired.
Makes 2 to 4 servings

*Fettuccine can be dried and stored at this point. Hang fettuccine strips over pasta rack or clean broom handle covered with plastic wrap and propped between 2 chairs. Dry for at least 3 hours; store in airtight container at room temperature up to 4 days. To serve, cook fettuccine in large pot of boiling salted water 3 to 4 minutes just until tender. Drain in colander.

Garlic-Onion Sauce

12 large cloves fresh garlic
½ cup butter
1 tablespoon olive oil
1 pound Vidalia or other sweet onions, sliced
1 tablespoon honey (optional)
¼ cup Marsala wine

1. To quickly peel garlic cloves, trim off the ends. Drop the cloves into boiling water. Boil 5 to 10 seconds. Remove with slotted spoon and plunge into cold water. Drain. The skins will slip off the cloves. With chef's knife, chop garlic to equal ⅓ cup.

2. Heat butter and oil in large skillet over medium heat. Add onions and garlic; cover and cook until soft. Add honey; reduce heat to low. Cook, uncovered, 30 minutes, stirring occasionally. Add wine; cook 5 to 10 minutes. *Makes about 2¼ cups*

Step 8. Kneading dough.

Step 9. Checking thickness of dough.

*Hanging pasta on pasta rack to dry.

Angel Hair Pasta with Red Chili Sauce

2 cups all-purpose flour
1/4 teaspoon salt
3 eggs
1 tablespoon milk
1 teaspoon olive oil
  Red Chili Sauce (page 34)
1/2 cup grated Parmesan cheese

1. Place flour, salt, eggs, milk and oil in food processor; process until dough forms. Shape into ball.

2. Place dough on lightly floured surface; flatten slightly. Cut dough into 4 pieces. Wrap 3 dough pieces in plastic wrap; set aside.

3. To knead by pasta machine, set rollers of pasta machine at widest setting (position 1).* Feed unwrapped dough piece through flat rollers by turning handle. (Dough may crumble slightly at first but will hold together after 2 to 3 rollings.)

4. Lightly flour dough strip; fold strip into thirds. Feed through rollers again. Continue process 7 to 10 times until dough is smooth and elastic.

5. To roll out dough by machine, reduce setting to position 3. Feed dough strip through rollers. Without folding strip into thirds, repeat on position 5 and 6. Let dough rest 5 to 10 minutes until slightly dry.

*Follow manufacturer's directions for appropriate method of rolling pasta if position settings are different. To make pasta by hand, see Spinach-Garlic Pasta with Garlic-Onion Sauce (page 30).

continued on page 34

Step 1. Preparing pasta dough in food processor.

Step 3. Kneading pasta dough in a pasta machine.

Step 4. Folding dough into thirds.

Angel Hair Pasta with Red Chili Sauce, continued

6. Attach handle to angel hair pasta roller and feed dough through.** Repeat kneading and rolling with reserved dough pieces.

7. Cook pasta in large pot of boiling salted water 1 to 2 minutes just until tender; remove from heat. Drain in colander.

8. Prepare Red Chili Sauce.

9. Toss sauce over pasta. Add cheese; toss well to coat.

Makes 4 to 6 servings

**Angel hair pasta can be dried and stored at this point. Hang pasta strips over pasta rack or clean broom handle covered with plastic wrap and propped between 2 chairs. (Technique on page 32.) Or, twirl pasta into nests and place on clean kitchen towel. Dry for at least 3 hours; store in airtight container at room temperature up to 4 days. Cook pasta in large pot of boiling salted water 3 to 4 minutes just until al dente. Drain in colander.

Red Chili Sauce

2 small red hot chili peppers***
6 tablespoons butter or margarine
4 green onions, thinly sliced
½ medium red bell pepper, minced
3 cloves garlic, minced (page 26)
3 tablespoons minced fresh parsley (page 38)
½ teaspoon salt
⅛ teaspoon black pepper

***Chili peppers can sting and irritate the skin; wear rubber gloves when handling peppers and do not touch eyes. Wash your hands after handling chili peppers.

1. Rinse chili peppers; pat dry with paper towels. Cut peppers into halves with utility knife. Scrape out seeds. Then chop with chef's knife until peppers are in uniform small pieces.

2. Heat butter in large skillet over medium-high heat. Add chili peppers, onions, bell pepper and garlic. Cook and stir 2 minutes or until onions are soft.

3. Remove from heat. Stir in parsley, salt and black pepper.

Makes about ³/₄ cup

Step 6. Cutting pasta with pasta machine.

Red Chili Sauce: Step 1. Scraping seeds from chili peppers.

Creamy Chicken and Red Pepper Pasta

¼ cup pine nuts or coarsely chopped walnuts
3 tablespoons vegetable oil, divided
1½ pounds boneless skinless chicken thighs
Salt and black pepper
1 pound fettuccine
¼ cup butter or margarine
3 cloves garlic, minced (page 26)
2 tablespoons all-purpose flour
1½ cups half-and-half
½ cup chicken broth
½ cup prepared roasted red peppers, drained and sliced
¼ cup sliced pitted ripe olives
⅓ cup grated Romano cheese

1. To toast pine nuts, heat 1 tablespoon oil in small skillet over medium-low heat. Add pine nuts; cook and stir 30 to 45 seconds until light brown, shaking pan constantly. Remove with slotted spoon; drain on paper towels.

2. Sprinkle chicken with salt and black pepper. Heat remaining 2 tablespoons oil in large skillet over medium-high heat. Add chicken and cook 12 to 15 minutes until browned on both sides and no longer pink in center.

3. Remove chicken from skillet. Refrigerate until cool enough to handle. Cut into bite-size pieces.

4. Cook pasta according to package directions. Rinse under warm running water; drain.

5. Melt butter in medium saucepan over medium heat. Add garlic; cook and stir until golden. Stir in flour until smooth. Cook 1 minute. Gradually stir in half-and-half and broth. Bring to a boil over medium heat; continue boiling 3 to 4 minutes or until slightly thickened and reduced.

6. Place fettuccine in large bowl. Add chicken, pine nuts, peppers and olives. Toss gently to coat. Pour sauce over fettuccine; toss gently. Add cheese and salt and black pepper to taste; toss. Garnish as desired.

Makes 4 main-dish or 8 appetizer servings

Step 1. Toasting pine nuts.

Step 2. Cutting into chicken to test doneness.

Step 3. Cutting chicken into bite-size pieces.

Scallops with Vermicelli

Fresh parsley
1 pound bay scallops
2 tablespoons lemon juice
12 ounces vermicelli
2 tablespoons olive oil
2 tablespoons butter, divided
1 medium onion, chopped
   (page 26)
1 clove garlic, minced (page 26)
1 can (14½ ounces) Italian
   tomatoes, undrained and
   cut up
2 tablespoons chopped fresh basil
   or 1 teaspoon dried basil,
   crushed
¼ teaspoon dried oregano leaves,
   crushed
¼ teaspoon dried thyme leaves,
   crushed
2 tablespoons heavy cream
   Dash ground nutmeg

1. To chop parsley, place parsley in 1-cup measuring cup. Snip enough parsley with kitchen scissors to measure 2 tablespoons. Set aside.

2. Rinse scallops. Combine scallops, parsley and lemon juice in glass dish. Cover; marinate in refrigerator while preparing sauce.

3. Cook pasta according to package directions. Drain in colander.

4. Heat oil and 1 tablespoon butter in large skillet over medium-high heat. Cook and stir onion and garlic in hot oil mixture until onion is tender.

5. Add tomatoes with juice, basil, oregano and thyme. Reduce heat to low. Cover; simmer 30 minutes, stirring occasionally.

6. Drain scallops. Cook and stir scallops in remaining 1 tablespoon butter in another large skillet over medium heat until scallops are opaque, about 2 minutes.

7. Stir tomato mixture, cream and nutmeg into scallop mixture.

8. Pour sauce over vermicelli in large bowl; toss gently to coat. Garnish as desired.

Makes 4 servings

Step 1. Chopping parsley with scissors.

Step 5. Adding tomatoes to skillet.

Step 6. Cooking and stirring scallops.

Crabmeat with Herbs and Pasta

1 clove garlic
  Fresh parsley
6 ounces crabmeat
$\frac{1}{2}$ package (8 ounces) vermicelli
$\frac{1}{3}$ cup olive oil
3 tablespoons butter or
  margarine
1 small onion, minced (page 26)
1 carrot, shredded
$\frac{1}{4}$ cup chopped fresh basil *or* 2
  teaspoons dried basil leaves,
  crushed
1 tablespoon lemon juice
$\frac{1}{2}$ cup coarsely chopped pine nuts
  (optional)
$\frac{1}{2}$ teaspoon salt

1. To mince garlic, trim ends of garlic clove. Slightly crush clove under flat side of chef's knife blade; peel away skin. Chop with chef's knife until garlic is minced. Set aside.

2. To chop parsley, place parsley in 1-cup measuring cup. Snip enough parsley with kitchen scissors to measure 2 tablespoons. Set aside.

3. Pick out and discard any shell or cartilage from crabmeat. Flake with fork. Set aside.

4. Cook pasta according to package directions. Drain in colander.

5. Heat oil and butter in large skillet over medium-high heat. Cook and stir garlic, onion and carrot in hot oil mixture until vegetables are tender, but not brown.

6. Reduce heat to medium. Stir in parsley, crabmeat, basil and lemon juice. Cook 4 minutes, stirring constantly. Stir in pine nuts and salt.

7. Pour sauce over vermicelli in large bowl; toss gently to coat. Garnish as desired.

Makes 4 servings

Step 1. Crushing garlic to remove skin.

Step 2. Chopping parsley with scissors.

Step 3. Picking out shell or cartilage from crabmeat.

Pasta Delight

12 ounces penne pasta
1 shallot
1 medium tomato
1 tablespoon olive oil
1 medium zucchini, sliced
2 cloves garlic, minced (page 26)
2 tablespoons chopped fresh basil
  or 1 teaspoon dried basil,
  crushed
2 tablespoons grated Parmesan
  cheese

1. Cook pasta according to package directions. Drain in colander.

2. Remove papery outer skin from shallot. Cut off root end. Chop with utility knife. Set aside.

3. Cut tomato into halves. Remove stem. Scrape out seeds with spoon. Chop into small pieces. Set aside.

4. Heat oil in large skillet over medium-high heat. Cook and stir zucchini in hot oil until slightly softened.

5. Reduce heat to medium. Add shallot and garlic; cook 1 minute.

6. Add tomato; cook and stir 45 seconds.

7. Add basil and cheese. Pour vegetable mixture over penne in large bowl; toss gently to mix.   *Makes 4 to 6 servings*

Step 2. Removing papery outer skin from shallot.

Step 3. Scraping out seeds from tomato.

Step 5. Cooking shallot and garlic with zucchini.

Pasta and Broccoli

1 **bunch broccoli**
1 **package (16 ounces) ziti macaroni**
2 **tablespoons olive oil**
1 **clove garlic, minced (page 26)**
³/₄ **cup (3 ounces) shredded American or mozzarella cheese**
¹/₂ **cup grated Parmesan cheese**
¹/₄ **cup butter**
¹/₄ **cup chicken broth**
3 **tablespoons white wine**

1. Trim leaves from broccoli stalks. Trim ends of stalks. Cut broccoli into flowerets by removing each head to include a small piece of the stem. Peel stalks, then cut into 1-inch pieces.

2. To steam broccoli, bring 2 inches of water in large saucepan to a boil over high heat. Place broccoli in metal steamer into saucepan. Water should not touch broccoli. Cover pan; steam 10 minutes until broccoli is tender. Add water, as necessary, to prevent pan from boiling dry.

3. Cook pasta according to package directions. Drain in colander.

4. Heat oil in large skillet over medium-high heat. Cook and stir garlic in hot oil until golden.

5. Add broccoli; cook and stir 3 to 4 minutes. Add American cheese, Parmesan cheese, butter, broth and wine; stir. Reduce heat to low. Simmer until cheese melts.

6. Pour sauce over ziti in large bowl; toss gently to coat. Garnish as desired.

Makes 6 to 8 servings

Step 1. Cutting broccoli stalk into 1-inch pieces.

Step 2. Steaming broccoli.

Step 5. Stirring broccoli mixture.

Fusilli Pizzaiolo

8 ounces mushrooms
1 large red bell pepper
1 large green bell pepper
1 large yellow bell pepper
3 large shallots
1 package (16 ounces) fusilli or
  spaghetti
¼ cup olive oil
10 green onions, chopped
1 large onion, diced (page 26)
8 cloves garlic, coarsely chopped
½ cup chopped fresh basil *or* 2
  teaspoons dried basil leaves,
  crushed
2 tablespoons chopped fresh
  oregano *or* 1 teaspoon dried
  oregano, crushed
  Dash crushed red pepper
4 cups canned or fresh tomatoes,
  chopped (page 42)
  Salt and black pepper to taste
  Fresh basil sprigs and
  miniature plum tomatoes for
  garnish

1. Wipe mushrooms clean with damp paper towel. Cut thin piece from stem; discard. Cut mushrooms into slices with paring knife. Set aside.

2. Rinse bell peppers under cold running water. To seed pepper, stand on end on cutting board. Cut off sides in 3 to 4 lengthwise slices with utility knife. (Cut close to, but not through, stem.) Discard stem and seeds. Scrape out any remaining seeds. Rinse inside of pepper under cold running water, then cut into ¼-inch pieces. Set aside.

3. Remove papery outer skin from shallots. Cut off root end. Chop with chef's knife. Set aside.

4. Cook pasta according to package directions. Drain in colander.

5. Heat oil in large skillet over medium-high heat. Cook and stir mushrooms, bell peppers, shallots, onions, garlic, chopped basil, oregano and crushed red pepper in hot oil until lightly browned.

6. Add tomatoes with juice; bring to a boil. Reduce heat to low; simmer, uncovered, 20 minutes. Season to taste with salt and black pepper.

7. Place fusilli on plates. Spoon sauce over fusilli. Garnish, if desired.

Makes 6 to 8 servings

Step 1. Cutting mushrooms into slices.

Step 2. Cutting off sides of bell pepper.

Step 3. Removing papery outer skin from shallot.

Spinach Pesto

1 bunch fresh spinach
  Fresh parsley leaves
  Spaghetti, pasta twists or shells
²/₃ cup grated Parmesan cheese
¹/₂ cup walnut pieces
6 cloves fresh garlic, crushed
4 flat anchovy filets
1 tablespoon dried tarragon
  leaves, crushed
1 teaspoon dried basil leaves,
  crushed
1 teaspoon salt
¹/₂ teaspoon pepper
¹/₄ teaspoon anise or fennel seed
1 cup olive oil
  Mixed salad (optional)

1. Separate spinach into leaves. Swish in cold water. Repeat several times with fresh cold water to remove sand and grit. Pat dry with paper towels.

2. To remove stems from spinach leaves, fold each leaf in half, then with hand pull stem toward top of leaf. Discard stem. Chop leaves with chef's knife. Set aside.

3. For parsley, strip leaves from stems using hands. Pack leaves into measuring cup to equal 1 cup. Set aside.

4. Cook desired amount of pasta according to package directions. Drain in colander.

5. Place spinach, parsley, cheese, walnuts, garlic, anchovies, tarragon, basil, salt, pepper and anise seed in covered food processor. Process until mixture is smooth.

6. While processing, add oil in thin stream. Adjust seasonings, if desired.

7. Pour desired amount over pasta; toss gently to coat. Serve with mixed salad. Garnish as desired.   *Makes 2 cups*

Note: Sauce can be stored in the refrigerator in an airtight container up to 1 week.

Step 1. Washing spinach.

Step 2. Removing stem from spinach.

Step 6. Slowly adding oil to food processor.

Penne with Artichokes

1 package (10 ounces) frozen
   artichokes
1¼ cups water
  2 tablespoons lemon juice
12 ounces penne pasta
  2 tablespoons olive oil, divided
  5 cloves garlic, minced (page 26)
  2 ounces oil-packed sun-dried
    tomatoes, drained
  2 small dried hot red peppers,
    crushed
  2 tablespoons chopped parsley
    (page 38)
  ¼ teaspoon salt
  ¼ teaspoon pepper
  ¾ cup fresh bread crumbs
  1 tablespoon chopped garlic
  1 tablespoon grated Romano
    cheese

1. Cook artichokes in water and lemon juice in medium saucepan over medium heat until tender. Drain artichokes, reserving liquid. Let artichokes stand until cool enough to handle. Cut into quarters using paring knife.

2. Cook pasta according to package directions. Drain in colander.

3. Heat 1½ tablespoons oil in large skillet over medium-high heat. Cook and stir minced garlic in hot oil until golden.

4. Reduce heat to low. Add artichokes and tomatoes; simmer 1 minute. Stir in artichoke liquid, red peppers, parsley, salt and pepper. Simmer 5 minutes.

5. Meanwhile, heat remaining ½ tablespoon oil in small skillet over medium-high heat. Cook and stir bread crumbs and chopped garlic in hot oil until lightly browned.

6. Pour artichoke sauce over penne in large bowl; toss gently to coat. Sprinkle with bread crumb mixture and cheese.

Makes 4 to 6 servings

Step 1. Cutting artichokes into quarters.

Step 4. Adding artichoke liquid to skillet.

Step 5. Cooking and stirring bread crumbs and garlic.

Tacos in Pasta Shells

1 package (3 ounces) cream
    cheese with chives
18 jumbo pasta shells
1¼ pounds ground beef
1 teaspoon salt
1 teaspoon chili powder
2 tablespoons butter, melted
1 cup prepared taco sauce
1 cup (4 ounces) shredded
    Cheddar cheese
1 cup (4 ounces) shredded
    Monterey Jack cheese
1½ cups crushed tortilla chips
1 cup dairy sour cream
3 green onions, chopped
    Leaf lettuce, small pitted ripe
    olives and cherry tomatoes for
    garnish

1. Place cream cheese on opened package on cutting board. Cut cream cheese lengthwise into ½-inch slices with utility knife. Then cut crosswise into ½-inch pieces. Let stand at room temperature until softened.

2. Cook pasta according to package directions. Place in colander and rinse under warm running water. Drain well. Return to saucepan.

3. Preheat oven to 350°F. Butter 13 × 9-inch baking pan.

4. Cook beef in large skillet over medium-high heat until brown, stirring to separate meat; drain drippings.

5. Reduce heat to medium-low. Add cream cheese, salt and chili powder; simmer 5 minutes.

6. Toss shells with butter. Fill shells with beef mixture using spoon. Arrange shells in prepared pan. Pour taco sauce over each shell. Cover with foil.

7. Bake 15 minutes. Uncover; top with Cheddar cheese, Monterey Jack cheese and chips. Bake 15 minutes more or until bubbly. Top with sour cream and onions. Garnish, if desired.　　　　*Makes 4 to 6 servings*

Step 1. Cutting cream cheese into ½-inch pieces.

Step 5. Stirring cream cheese in skillet.

Step 6. Filling shells with beef mixture.

Spaghetti Rolls

1 package (8 ounces) manicotti
  shells
2 pounds ground beef
1 tablespoon onion powder
1 teaspoon salt
½ teaspoon pepper
2 cups spaghetti sauce, divided
1 cup (4 ounces) shredded pizza-
  flavored cheese blend or
  mozzarella cheese

1. Cook pasta according to package directions. Place in colander, then rinse under warm running water. Drain well.

2. Preheat oven to 350°F. Grease 13 × 9-inch baking pan.

3. Cook beef in large skillet over medium-high heat until brown, stirring to separate meat; drain drippings.

4. Stir in onion powder, salt and pepper. Stir in 1 cup spaghetti sauce; cool and set aside.

5. Reserve ½ cup ground beef mixture. Combine remaining beef mixture with cheese in large bowl. Fill shells with remaining beef mixture using spoon.

6. Arrange shells in prepared pan. Combine remaining spaghetti sauce with reserved beef mixture in small bowl; blend well. Pour over shells. Cover with foil.

7. Bake 20 to 30 minutes or until hot. Garnish as desired. *Makes 4 servings*

Step 1. Rinsing pasta under warm running water.

Step 3. Stirring ground beef to separate meat.

Step 5. Filling shells with beef texture.

Polish Reuben Casserole

1 medium onion
2 cans (16 ounces each) sauerkraut
2 cans (10 3/4 ounces each) condensed cream of mushroom soup
1 1/3 cups milk
1 tablespoon prepared mustard
1 package (8 ounces) medium-width noodles
1 1/2 pounds Polish sausage, cut into 1/2-inch pieces
2 cups (8 ounces) shredded Swiss cheese
3/4 cup whole wheat bread crumbs
2 tablespoons butter, melted

1. Preheat oven to 350°F. Grease 13 × 9-inch baking pan.

2. To chop onion, peel skin. Cut onion in half through the root with a utility knife. Place cut side down on cutting board. Holding knife horizontally, make cuts parallel to the board, almost to root end. Next, cut onion vertically into thin slices, holding onion with fingers to keep its shape, then turn onion and cut crosswise to root end. (The closer the cuts are, the finer the onion is chopped.) Repeat with remaining onion half.

3. Place sauerkraut in colander in sink. Rinse under cold running water. Press sauerkraut in colander with spoon to drain well.

4. Combine onion, soup, milk and mustard in medium bowl; blend well.

5. Spread sauerkraut in prepared pan. Top with uncooked noodles. Spoon soup mixture evenly over noodles. Top with sausage, then cheese.

6. Combine crumbs and butter in small bowl; sprinkle over top of casserole. Cover pan tightly with foil.

7. Bake 1 hour or until noodles are tender. Garnish as desired.

Makes 8 to 10 servings

Step 2. Chopping onion.

Step 3. Pressing sauerkraut with spoon to drain.

Step 5. Spreading soup mixture over casserole.

Beef Oriental

3 cups corkscrew pasta
7 green onions
2 to 3 ribs celery
8 mushrooms (optional)
1 package (20 ounces) frozen pea
    pods
1 pound ground beef
3 tablespoons soy sauce
¼ teaspoon ground ginger
1 can (8 ounces) tomato sauce
3 fresh tomatoes, cut into wedges
1 cup (4 ounces) shredded
    Cheddar cheese, divided
1 green pepper, cut into thin
    slices

1. Cook pasta according to package directions. Drain in colander. Set aside.

2. Remove roots from green onions. Cut green onions diagonally into 2-inch pieces.

3. Place celery flat side down on cutting board. Cut celery diagonally into 1-inch pieces.

4. Wipe mushrooms clean with damp paper towel. Cut thin piece from stem; discard. Cut mushrooms into slices with paring knife. (Technique on page 46).

5. To quickly thaw pea pods, place in colander. Rinse under hot water until no ice crystals remain and pea pods are easily separated. Drain well; pat dry with paper towel.

6. Cook beef, onions, soy sauce and ginger in wok over medium-high heat until meat is brown, stirring to separate meat.

7. Push mixture up the side of wok. Add celery and mushrooms; stir-fry 2 minutes. Push mixture up the side. Add pea pods and tomato sauce; cook 4 to 5 minutes, stirring every minute.

8. Add pasta, tomatoes and ¾ cup cheese. Stir gently to combine all ingredients. Cook 1 minute. Add green pepper; sprinkle remaining ¼ cup cheese over top. Reduce heat to low; cook until heated through.

Makes 4 servings

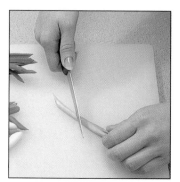

Step 2. Cutting green onions diagonally into 2-inch pieces.

Step 3. Cutting celery diagonally into 1-inch pieces.

Step 7. Stir-frying vegetables.

String Pie

8 ounces spaghetti
1 medium onion
1 pound ground beef
¼ cup chopped green pepper
1 jar (15½ ounces) spaghetti
  sauce
⅓ cup grated Parmesan cheese
2 eggs, beaten
2 teaspoons butter
1 cup cottage cheese
½ cup (2 ounces) shredded
  mozzarella cheese

1. Cook pasta according to package directions. Drain in colander.

2. To chop onion, peel skin. Cut onion in half through the root with a utility knife. Place cut side down on cutting board. Holding knife horizontally, make cuts parallel to the board, almost to root end. Next, cut onion vertically into thin slices, holding onion with fingers to keep its shape, then turn onion and cut crosswise to root end. (The closer the cuts are, the finer the onion is chopped.) Repeat with remaining onion half.

3. Preheat oven to 350°F.

4. Cook beef, onion and green pepper in large skillet over medium-high heat until meat is brown, stirring to separate meat; drain drippings. Stir in spaghetti sauce; mix well.

5. Combine spaghetti, Parmesan cheese, eggs and butter in large bowl; mix well. Place in bottom of 13×9-inch baking pan. Spread cottage cheese over top. Pour sauce mixture over cottage cheese. Sprinkle mozzarella over top of casserole.

6. Bake 20 minutes or until hot and cheese melts.

Makes 6 to 8 servings

Step 2. Chopping onion.

Step 4. Stirring ground beef to separate meat.

Step 5. Spreading cottage cheese over spaghetti sauce.

Sunday Supper Stuffed Shells

1 package (12 ounces) jumbo
   pasta shells
1 package (10 ounces) frozen
   chopped spinach
2 tablespoons olive oil
3 cloves fresh garlic, peeled
³/₄ pound ground veal
³/₄ pound ground pork
1 cup parsley, finely chopped
   (page 38)
1 cup bread crumbs
2 eggs, beaten
3 cloves fresh garlic, minced
   (page 26)
3 tablespoons grated Parmesan
   cheese
   Salt to taste
3 cups spaghetti sauce
   Sauteed zucchini slices
   (optional)

1. Cook pasta according to package directions. Place in colander and rinse under warm running water. Drain well.

2. Cook spinach according to package directions. Place in colander to drain. Let stand until cool enough to handle. Squeeze spinach with hands to remove excess moisture. Set aside.

3. Heat oil in large skillet over medium heat. Cook and stir whole garlic cloves in hot oil until garlic is lightly browned. Discard garlic.

4. Add veal and pork to skillet. Cook until lightly brown, stirring to separate meat; drain drippings. Cool slightly.

5. Preheat oven to 375°F. Grease 12 × 8-inch baking pan.

6. Combine spinach, parsley, bread crumbs, eggs, minced garlic and cheese in large bowl; blend well. Season to taste with salt. Add cooled meat mixture; blend well. Fill shells with meat mixture using spoon.

7. Spread about 1 cup of spaghetti sauce over bottom of prepared pan. Arrange shells in pan. Pour remaining sauce over shells. Cover with foil.

8. Bake 35 to 45 minutes or until bubbly. Serve with zucchini. Garnish as desired.

Makes 8 to 9 servings

Step 2. Squeezing spinach with hands to remove excess moisture.

Step 4. Stirring ground meat to separate meat.

Step 6. Filling shells with meat mixture.

Cheesy Chicken Roll-Ups

1 package (8 ounces) cream cheese
3 tablespoons sliced almonds
6 lasagna noodles
¼ cup butter
1 medium onion, diced (page 26)
4 ounces fresh mushrooms, sliced (page 46)
3 boneless skinless chicken breast halves, cut into bite-sized pieces (page 8)
¾ cup dry white wine
½ teaspoon dried tarragon leaves, crushed
½ teaspoon salt
½ teaspoon pepper
½ cup heavy cream
½ cup dairy sour cream
1½ cups (6 ounces) shredded Swiss cheese, divided
1 cup (4 ounces) shredded Muenster cheese, divided
Chopped parsley (optional) (page 38)

1. Place cream cheese on opened package on cutting board. Cut cream cheese lengthwise into ½-inch slices with utility knife. Then cut crosswise into ½-inch pieces; set aside. Let stand at room temperature until softened.

2. To toast almonds, spread on baking sheet. Bake in preheated 350°F oven 8 to 10 minutes or until golden brown, stirring frequently. Remove almonds from pan and cool; set aside. *Reduce oven temperature to 325°F.* Grease 13 × 9-inch baking pan; set aside.

3. Cook lasagna noodles according to package directions. Drain in colander. Rinse under warm running water; drain well. When cool enough to handle, cut noodles lengthwise into halves.

4. Melt butter in large skillet over medium-high heat. Cook and stir onion and mushrooms in hot butter until tender. Add chicken, wine, tarragon, salt and pepper; bring to a boil over high heat. Reduce heat to low. Simmer 10 minutes.

5. Curl each lasagna noodle half into a circle; arrange in prepared pan. With slotted spoon, fill center of lasagna rings with chicken mixture.

6. To remaining liquid in skillet, add cream cheese, heavy cream, sour cream, ¾ cup of Swiss cheese and ½ cup of Muenster cheese. Cook and stir over medium-low heat until cheese melts. *Do not boil.* Pour over lasagna rings. Sprinkle remaining cheeses and almonds on top.

7. Bake 35 minutes or until bubbly. Sprinkle with parsley. Garnish as desired.

Makes 6 servings

Step 1. Cutting cream cheese into ½-inch pieces.

Step 2. Toasting almonds.

Step 5. Filling noodle circle with chicken mixture.

Sweet Garlic with Chicken Pasta

1¼ **pounds boneless skinless chicken breast halves**
4 **ounces fresh plum tomatoes**
1 **package (16 ounces) bow tie pasta**
8 **ounces garlic**
5½ **tablespoons olive oil**
1½ **pounds shiitake mushrooms, sliced**
1 **cup chopped green onions**
1 **teaspoon crushed red pepper flakes**
2 **cups chicken broth**
4 **ounces cilantro, chopped, divided (see parsley, page 38)**

1. To grill chicken, heat single layer of coals in grill to medium. Oil hot grid to help prevent sticking. Grill chicken, on covered grill, 6 to 8 minutes until chicken is no longer pink in center, turning chicken over halfway through cooking.

2. Refrigerate grilled chicken until cool enough to handle. Cut chicken into ½-inch cubes. Set aside.

3. Cut tomatoes into halves. Remove stems. Scrape out seeds with spoon. Chop into small pieces to equal 2 cups. Set aside. (Technique on page 42.)

4. Cook pasta according to package directions. Drain in colander.

5. To peel garlic cloves, trim off ends. Drop cloves into boiling water. Boil 5 to 10 seconds. Remove with slotted spoon; plunge into cold water. Drain. The skins will slip off cloves. Chop with chef's knife until garlic is in very small uniform pieces.

6. Heat oil in large skillet over medium-high heat. Cook and stir garlic in hot oil until lightly browned. Add tomatoes, mushrooms, green onions and red pepper flakes. Cook and stir 2 minutes.

7. Add broth; simmer mixture to reduce slightly. Add chicken, pasta and half of cilantro; heat through. Garnish with remaining cilantro. *Makes 6 to 8 servings*

Step 1. Grilling chicken.

Step 2. Cutting chicken into ½-inch pieces.

Step 6. Adding vegetables to skillet.

Shrimp in Angel Hair Pasta Casserole

1 pound medium raw shrimp
  Fresh parsley
2 eggs
1 cup half-and-half
1 cup plain yogurt
1/2 cup (4 ounces) shredded Swiss
  cheese
1/3 cup crumbled feta cheese
1/4 cup chopped fresh basil *or*
  2 teaspoons dried basil leaves,
  crushed
1 teaspoon dried oregano leaves,
  crushed
1 package (9 ounces) fresh angel
  hair pasta
1 jar (16 ounces) mild, thick and
  chunky salsa
1/2 cup (4 ounces) shredded
  Monterey Jack cheese
  Snow peas and plum tomatoes
  stuffed with cottage cheese for
  garnish

1. To peel shrimp, remove the legs by gently pulling them off the shell. Loosen shell with fingers, then slide off.

2. To devein shrimp, cut a shallow slit along back of shrimp with paring knife. Lift out intestinal vein. (You may find this easier to do under cold running water.) If desired, this step may be omitted.

3. To chop parsley, place parsley in 1-cup measuring cup. Snip enough parsley with kitchen scissors to measure 1/3 cup. Set aside. (Technique on page 38.)

4. Preheat oven to 350°F. Grease 12 × 8-inch baking pan with 1 tablespoon butter.

5. Combine parsley, eggs, half-and-half, yogurt, Swiss cheese, feta cheese, basil and oregano in medium bowl; mix well.

6. Spread half the pasta on bottom of prepared pan. Cover with salsa. Add half the shrimp. Cover with remaining pasta. Spread egg mixture over pasta and top with remaining shrimp. Sprinkle Monterey Jack cheese over top.

7. Bake 30 minutes or until bubbly. Let stand 10 minutes. Garnish, if desired.

Makes 6 servings

Step 1. Removing shell from shrimp.

Step 2. Deveining shrimp.

Step 6. Spreading egg mixture over pasta.

Shrimp Noodle Supreme

1 package (3 ounces) cream cheese
1½ pounds medium raw shrimp
1 package (8 ounces) spinach noodles
½ cup butter, softened
  Salt and pepper to taste
1 can (10¾ ounces) condensed cream of mushroom soup
1 cup dairy sour cream
½ cup half-and-half
½ cup mayonnaise
1 tablespoon chopped chives
1 tablespoon chopped parsley (page 38)
½ teaspoon Dijon-style mustard
¾ cup (3 ounces) shredded sharp Cheddar cheese
  Lemon slices and paprika for garnish

1. Place cream cheese on opened package on cutting board. Cut cream cheese lengthwise into ½-inch slices with utility knife. Then cut crosswise into ½-inch pieces; set aside. Let stand at room temperature until softened.

2. To peel shrimp, remove the legs by gently pulling them off the shell. Loosen shell with fingers, then slide shell off.

3. To devein shrimp, cut a shallow slit along back of shrimp with paring knife. Lift out intestinal vein. (You may find this easier to do under cold running water.) If desired, this step may be omitted.

4. Cook pasta according to package directions. Drain in colander.

5. Preheat oven to 325°F. Grease 13 × 9-inch glass casserole.

6. Combine cream cheese and noodles in medium bowl. Spread noodle mixture in bottom of prepared dish.

7. Heat butter in large skillet over medium-high heat. Cook shrimp in hot butter about 5 minutes or until shrimp turn pink and opaque. Season to taste with salt and pepper. Place shrimp on noodles.

8. Combine soup, sour cream, half-and-half, mayonnaise, chives, parsley and mustard in another medium bowl. Spread over shrimp. Sprinkle Cheddar cheese over top of casserole.

9. Bake 25 minutes or until hot and cheese melts. Garnish, if desired.

Makes 6 servings

Step 1. Cutting cream cheese into ½-inch pieces.

Step 2. Removing shell from shrimp.

Step 3. Deveining shrimp.

Saucy Mediterranean Frittata

Tomato Sauce (recipe follows)
1 medium tomato
1 tablespoon olive oil
1 small onion, chopped (page 26)
1 tablespoon finely chopped fresh basil *or* 1 teaspoon dried basil leaves, crushed
1/4 teaspoon dried oregano leaves, crushed
1/3 cup cooked orzo
1/3 cup chopped pitted ripe olives
8 eggs
1/2 teaspoon salt
1/8 teaspoon pepper
2 tablespoons butter
1/2 cup (2 ounces) shredded mozzarella cheese

1. Prepare Tomato Sauce.

2. Cut tomato into halves. Remove stem. Scrape out seeds with spoon. Chop into small pieces. Set aside.

3. Heat oil in ovenproof 10-inch skillet over medium-high heat. Cook and stir onion in hot oil until tender. Add tomato, basil and oregano; cook and stir 3 minutes. Stir in orzo and olives; remove from skillet and set aside.

4. Beat eggs, salt and pepper in medium bowl with electric mixer at low speed. Stir in tomato mixture; set aside.

5. Melt butter in same skillet over medium heat. Add egg mixture; top with cheese. Reduce heat to low. Cook 8 to 10 minutes or until bottom and most of middle is set.

6. Place skillet on rack 4 inches from broiler. Broil 1 to 2 minutes or until top is browned. Cut into wedges; serve with Tomato Sauce. Garnish as desired. Cut into wedges to serve.

Makes 4 to 6 servings

Step 2. Scraping out seeds from tomatoes.

Step 5. Cooking frittata until bottom of mixture is almost set.

Tomato Sauce

1 can (8 ounces) tomato sauce
1 teaspoon minced dried onion
1/4 teaspoon dried basil leaves, crushed
1/4 teaspoon dried oregano leaves, crushed
1/8 teaspoon minced dried garlic
1/8 teaspoon pepper

Combine all sauce ingredients in small saucepan. Bring to a boil over high heat. Reduce heat to low. Simmer, uncovered, over medium-low heat 5 minutes, stirring often. Set aside; keep warm. *Makes about 1 cup*

Spinach Stuffed Manicotti

1 package (10 ounces) frozen
    spinach
8 manicotti shells
2 eggs
1½ teaspoons olive oil
1 teaspoon dried rosemary
    leaves, crushed
1 teaspoon dried sage leaves,
    crushed
1 teaspoon dried oregano leaves,
    crushed
1 teaspoon dried thyme leaves,
    crushed
1 teaspoon chopped garlic
1½ cups fresh or canned tomatoes,
    chopped
4 ounces ricotta cheese
1 slice whole wheat bread, torn
    into coarse crumbs
    Yellow pepper rings and sage
    sprig for garnish

1. Cook spinach according to package directions. Place in colander to drain. Let stand until cool enough to handle. Squeeze spinach with hands to remove excess moisture. Set aside.

2. Cook pasta. Drain in colander. Rinse under warm running water; drain.

3. To separate egg whites from yolks, gently tap egg in center against a hard surface, such as the side of a bowl. Holding a shell half in each hand, transfer yolk back and forth between shell halves. Allow the white to drip down between the 2 halves into a bowl.

4. When all the white has dripped into bowl, place the yolk in another bowl. Place white in a third bowl. Repeat with remaining egg. Beat the 2 egg whites lightly with fork. Store egg yolks, covered with water, in airtight container. Refrigerate up to 2 days.

5. Preheat oven to 350°F.

6. Heat oil in small saucepan over medium heat. Cook and stir rosemary, sage, oregano, thyme and garlic in hot oil about 1 minute. Do not let herbs turn brown. Add tomatoes; reduce heat to low. Simmer, uncovered, 10 minutes, stirring occasionally.

7. Combine spinach, cheese and crumbs in bowl. Fold in egg whites. Fill shells with spinach mixture using spoon.

8. Place one third of tomato mixture on bottom of 13×9-inch baking pan. Arrange manicotti in pan. Pour tomato mixture over top. Cover with foil.

9. Bake 30 minutes or until bubbly. Garnish, if desired. *Makes 4 servings*

Step 1. Squeezing spinach with hands to remove excess moisture.

Step 3. Separating egg yolk from the whites.

Step 7. Filling shells with spinach mixture.

Rigatoni with Four Cheeses

12 ounces rigatoni
3 cups milk
1 tablespoon chopped carrot
1 tablespoon chopped celery
1 tablespoon chopped onion
2 parsley sprigs
1/2 bay leaf
1/4 teaspoon black peppercorns
1/4 teaspoon hot pepper sauce
   Dash ground nutmeg
1/4 cup butter
1/4 cup all-purpose flour
1/2 cup grated Wisconsin
   Parmesan cheese
1/4 cup grated Wisconsin Romano
   cheese
1 1/2 cups (6 ounces) shredded
   Wisconsin Cheddar cheese
1 1/2 cups (6 ounces) shredded
   Wisconsin mozzarella cheese
1/4 teaspoon chili powder

1. Cook pasta according to package directions. Drain in colander.

2. Combine milk, carrot, celery, onion, parsley, bay leaf, peppercorns, hot pepper sauce and nutmeg in medium saucepan. Bring to a boil over medium heat. Reduce heat to low. Simmer, uncovered, 10 minutes. Strain; reserve milk.

3. Preheat oven to 350°F. Butter 2-quart casserole.

4. Melt butter in another medium saucepan over medium heat. Stir in flour. Gradually stir in reserved milk. Cook, stirring constantly, until thickened. Remove from heat. Add Parmesan and Romano cheeses, stirring until blended.

5. Combine rigatoni and sauce in large bowl; toss gently to coat. Combine Cheddar and mozzarella cheeses in medium bowl. Place half the pasta mixture in prepared casserole. Sprinkle cheese mixture over top; place remaining pasta mixture on top. Sprinkle with chili powder.

6. Bake 25 minutes or until bubbly. Garnish as desired. *Makes 6 servings*

Step 2. Straining milk.

Step 4. Stirring milk into butter-flour mixture.

Step 5. Tossing rigatoni with sauce to coat.

Wisconsin Swiss Linguine Tart

French bread
½ cup butter, divided
2 cloves garlic, finely chopped (page 26)
8 ounces fresh linguine
3 tablespoons all-purpose flour
1 teaspoon salt
¼ teaspoon white pepper
Dash ground nutmeg
2½ cups milk
¼ cup grated Wisconsin Parmesan cheese
2 eggs, beaten
2 cups (8 ounces) shredded Wisconsin Swiss cheese, divided
⅓ cup sliced green onions
2 tablespoons minced fresh basil or 1 teaspoon dry basil leaves, crushed
2 plum tomatoes, each cut lengthwise into eighths

1. Preheat oven to 400°F.

2. Cut French bread crosswise with serrated knife into 30 (¼-inch) slices.

3. Melt ¼ cup butter in small saucepan over medium heat. Add garlic; cook 1 minute.

4. Brush 10-inch pie plate with butter mixture. Line bottom and side of pie plate with bread, allowing up to 1-inch overhang. Brush bread with remaining butter mixture. Bake 5 minutes or until lightly browned. Reduce oven temperature to 350°F.

5. Cook pasta in Dutch oven in boiling salted water 1 to 2 minutes just until tender. Drain in colander.

6. Melt remaining ¼ cup butter in medium saucepan over medium heat. Stir in flour, salt, pepper and nutmeg. Gradually stir in milk; cook, stirring constantly, until thickened. Add Parmesan cheese. Stir some of the sauce into eggs, then stir back into sauce. Set aside.

7. Combine linguine, 1¼ cups Swiss cheese, onions and basil in large bowl. Pour sauce over linguine mixture; toss to coat.

8. Pour mixture into crust. Arrange tomatoes on top; sprinkle with remaining ¾ cup Swiss cheese.

9. Bake in 350°F. oven 25 minutes or until warm; let stand 5 minutes before cutting. Garnish as desired.   *Makes 8 servings*

Step 4. Placing bread slices around edge of pie plate.

Step 6. Stirring some of the hot sauce into eggs.

Lasagna Supreme

8 ounces lasagna noodles
1/2 pound ground beef
1/2 pound mild Italian sausage, casings removed
1 medium onion, chopped (page 26)
2 cloves garlic, minced
1 can (14 1/2 ounces) whole peeled tomatoes, undrained and cut up
1 can (6 ounces) tomato paste
2 teaspoons dried basil leaves, crushed
1 teaspoon dried marjoram, crushed
1 can (4 ounces) sliced mushrooms, drained
2 eggs
1 pound cream-style cottage cheese
3/4 cup Parmesan cheese, divided
2 tablespoons parsley flakes
1/2 teaspoon salt
1/2 teaspoon pepper
2 cups (8 ounces) shredded Cheddar cheese
3 cups (12 ounces) shredded mozzarella cheese
Mixed salad (optional)

1. Cook lasagna noodles according to package directions. Drain in colander.

2. Cook meats, onion and garlic in large skillet over medium-high heat until meat is brown, stirring to separate meat. Drain drippings.

3. Add tomatoes with juice, tomato paste, basil and marjoram. Reduce heat to low. Cover; simmer 15 minutes, stirring often. Stir in mushrooms; set aside.

4. Preheat oven to 375°F.

5. Beat eggs in large bowl; add cottage cheese, 1/2 cup Parmesan cheese, parsley, salt and pepper. Mix well.

6. Place half the noodles in bottom of 13 × 9-inch baking pan. Spread half the cottage cheese mixture over noodles, then half the meat mixture and half the Cheddar cheese and mozzarella cheese.

7. Repeat layers. Sprinkle with remaining 1/4 cup Parmesan cheese.

8. Bake lasagna 40 to 45 minutes or until bubbly. Let stand 10 minutes before cutting. Serve with mixed salad.

Makes 8 to 10 servings

Note: Lasagna may be assembled, covered and refrigerated. Bake, uncovered, in preheated 375°F oven 60 minutes or until bubbly.

Step 3. Stirring mushrooms into skillet.

Step 6. Layering lasagna.

Spetzque

9 lasagna noodles
1 small onion
2 pounds ground beef
1 can (4½ ounces) chopped ripe
  olives, drained
1 can (4 ounces) mushroom stems
  and pieces, drained
1 jar (16 ounces) spaghetti sauce
  Dash pepper
  Dash dried oregano leaves,
  crushed
  Dash Italian seasoning
1¼ cups frozen corn, thawed
1¼ cups frozen peas, thawed
2 cups (8 ounces) shredded
  mozzarella cheese

1. Cook lasagna noodles according to package directions. Drain in colander.

2. To chop onion, peel skin. Cut onion in half through the root with a utility knife. Place cut side down on cutting board. Holding knife horizontally, make cuts parallel to the board, almost to root end. Next, cut onion vertically into thin slices, holding onion with fingers to keep its shape, then turn onion and cut crosswise to root end. (The closer the cuts are, the finer the onion is chopped.) Repeat with remaining onion half.

3. Cook beef in large skillet over medium-high heat until meat is brown, stirring to separate meat; drain drippings.

4. Add olives, mushrooms and onion. Cook, stirring occasionally, until vegetables are tender. Add spaghetti sauce, pepper, oregano and Italian seasoning. Heat through, stirring occasionally; set aside.

5. Preheat oven to 350°F.

6. Place 3 noodles in bottom of 13 × 9-inch baking pan. Spread half the beef mixture over noodles, then half the corn and peas.

7. Repeat layers ending with noodles.

8. Bake lasagna 25 minutes. Sprinkle with cheese; bake 5 minutes more or until bubbly. Let stand 10 minutes before cutting. Garnish as desired. *Makes 6 servings*

Step 2. Chopping onion.

Step 4. Stirring spaghetti sauce into meat mixture.

Step 6. Layering lasagna.

Lazy Lasagna

1 **pound ground beef**
1 **jar (32 ounces) spaghetti sauce**
1 **pound cottage cheese**
8 **ounces sour cream**
8 **lasagna noodles**
3 **packages (6 ounces each) sliced**
   mozzarella cheese (12 slices)
½ **cup grated Parmesan cheese**
1 **cup water**

1. Cook beef in large skillet over medium-high heat until meat is brown, stirring to separate meat; drain drippings.

2. Add spaghetti sauce. Reduce heat to low. Heat through, stirring occasionally; set aside.

3. Preheat oven to 350°F.

4. Combine cottage cheese and sour cream in medium bowl; blend well.

5. Spoon 1½ cups of meat sauce in bottom of 13 × 9-inch baking pan. Place 4 of uncooked noodles over sauce, then half the cheese mixture, 4 slices of mozzarella cheese, half the remaining meat sauce and ¼ cup of Parmesan cheese.

6. Repeat layers starting with the uncooked noodles. Top with remaining 4 slices of mozzarella cheese. Pour water around the sides of the pan. Cover tightly with foil.

7. Bake lasagna 1 hour. Uncover; bake 20 minutes more or until bubbly. Let stand 15 to 20 minutes before cutting. Garnish, if desired.

Makes 8 to 10 servings

Step 2. Stirring spaghetti sauce into meat.

Step 5. Layering lasagna.

Step 6. Pouring water around lasagna.

Luscious Vegetarian Lasagna

8 ounces lasagna noodles
1 can (14¹/₂ ounces) whole peeled tomatoes, undrained and coarsely chopped
1 can (12 ounces) tomato sauce
1 teaspoon dried oregano leaves, crushed
1 teaspoon dried basil leaves, crushed
Dash black pepper
2 tablespoons olive oil
1 large onion, chopped (page 26)
1¹/₂ teaspoons minced garlic
2 small zucchini cut into bite-size pieces (page 28)
1 large carrot, chopped
1 green bell pepper, cut into ¹/₄-inch pieces (page 46)
8 ounces mushrooms, sliced
1 cup (4 ounces) shredded mozzarella cheese
2 cups 1% milk-fat cottage cheese
1 cup grated Parmesan or Romano cheese
Parsley sprigs for garnish

Substitution: Other vegetables may be added or substituted for the ones listed above.

1. Cook lasagna according to package directions. Drain in colander.

2. Place tomatoes with juice, tomato sauce, oregano, basil and black pepper in medium saucepan. Bring to a boil over high heat. Reduce heat to low. Simmer, uncovered, 6 to 10 minutes.

3. Heat oil in large skillet over medium-high heat. Cook and stir onion and garlic in hot oil until onion is golden. Add zucchini, carrot, bell pepper and mushrooms. Cook and stir 5 to 10 minutes or until vegetables are tender. Stir vegetables into tomato mixture; bring to a boil. Reduce heat to low. Simmer, uncovered, 15 minutes.

4. Preheat oven to 350°F.

5. Combine mozzarella, cottage and Parmesan cheeses in large bowl; blend well.

6. Spoon about 1 cup sauce in bottom of 12 × 8-inch baking pan. Place a layer of noodles over sauce, then half the cheese mixture and half the remaining sauce.

7. Repeat layers of noodles, cheese mixture and sauce.

8. Bake lasagna 30 to 45 minutes or until bubbly. Let stand 10 minutes. Garnish with parsley.   *Makes 6 to 8 servings*

Step 2. Stirring spices into tomato mixture.

Step 3. Adding vegetables to skillet.

Step 6. Layering lasagna.

Apple Lasagna

8 lasagna noodles
2 cups (8 ounces) shredded
   Cheddar cheese
1 cup ricotta cheese
1 egg, lightly beaten
¼ cup granulated sugar
1 teaspoon almond extract
2 cans (20 ounces each) apple pie
   filling
6 tablespoons all-purpose flour
6 tablespoons packed brown
   sugar
¼ cup uncooked quick-cooking
   oats
½ teaspoon ground cinnamon
   Dash ground nutmeg
3 tablespoons margarine
1 cup sour cream
⅓ cup packed brown sugar

1. Cook lasagna noodles according to package directions. Drain in colander.

2. Preheat oven to 350°F. Grease 13 × 9-inch baking pan.

3. Combine Cheddar cheese, ricotta cheese, egg, granulated sugar and almond extract in medium bowl; blend well.

4. Spread 1 can apple pie filling over bottom of prepared pan. Layer half the noodles over filling, then spread cheese mixture over noodles. Top with remaining noodles, then remaining can of apple pie filling.

5. Combine flour, 6 tablespoons brown sugar, oats, cinnamon and nutmeg in small bowl. Cut in margarine with pastry blender or 2 knives until crumbly. Sprinkle over apple pie filling.

6. Bake lasagna 45 minutes. Cool 15 minutes.

7. Meanwhile, prepare garnish by blending sour cream and ⅓ cup brown sugar in small bowl until smooth. Cover; refrigerate.

8. To serve, cut lasagna into squares and garnish with sour cream mixture.

Makes 12 to 15 servings

Step 3. Combining cheese.

Step 4. Layering lasagna.

Step 5. Cutting margarine into oat mixture.

Seafood Lasagna

1 package (8 ounces) cream
   cheese
1 package (16 ounces) lasagna
   noodles
1 large onion
1 clove garlic
1/2 pound medium raw shrimp
1/2 pound flounder fillets
1/2 pound bay scallops
2 tablespoons butter or
   margarine
1 1/2 cups cream-style cottage
   cheese
2 teaspoons dried basil leaves,
   crushed
1/2 teaspoon salt
1/8 teaspoon pepper
1 egg, lightly beaten
2 cans (10 3/4 ounces each) cream
   of mushroom soup
1/3 cup milk
1/2 cup dry white wine
1 cup (4 ounces) shredded
   mozzarella cheese
2 tablespoons grated Parmesan
   cheese

1. Place cream cheese on opened package on cutting board. Cut cream cheese lengthwise into 1/2-inch slices with utility knife. Then cut crosswise into 1/2-inch pieces; set aside. Let stand at room temperature until softened.

2. Cook lasagna noodles according to package directions. Drain in colander.

3. To chop onion, peel skin. Cut onion in half with a utility knife. Place cut side down on cutting board. Holding knife horizontally, make cuts parallel to the board, almost to root end. Next, cut onion vertically into thin slices, holding onion with fingers to keep its shape, then turn onion and cut crosswise to root end. (The closer the cuts are, the finer the onion is chopped.) Repeat with remaining onion half.

4. To mince garlic, trim ends of garlic clove. Slightly crush clove under flat side of chef's knife blade; peel away skin. Chop garlic with chef's knife until minced (uniform fine pieces). Set aside.

continued on page 92

Step 1. Cutting cream cheese into 1/2-inch pieces.

Step 3. Chopping onion.

Step 4. Crushing garlic to remove skin.

Seafood Lasagna, continued

5. To peel shrimp, remove the legs by gently pulling them off the shell. Loosen shell with fingers, then slide off.

6. To devein shrimp, with paring knife cut a shallow slit along back of shrimp. Lift out intestinal vein. (You may find this easier to do under cold running water.) If desired, this step may be omitted. Set aside.

7. Rinse fish fillets and scallops. Pat dry with paper towels. Cut fillets into ½-inch cubes.

8. Melt butter in large skillet over medium heat. Cook onion in hot butter until tender, stirring frequently. Stir in cream cheese, cottage cheese, basil, salt and pepper; mix well. Stir in egg; set aside.

9. Combine soup, milk and garlic in large bowl until well blended. Stir in scallops, fillets, shrimp and wine.

10. Preheat oven to 350°F. Grease 13×9-inch baking pan.

11. Place a layer of noodles in prepared pan, overlapping the noodles. Spread half the cheese mixture over noodles. Place a layer of noodles over cheese mixture and top with half the seafood mixture.

12. Repeat layers. Sprinkle with mozzarella and Parmesan cheeses.

13. Bake 45 minutes or until bubbly. Let stand 10 minutes before cutting.

Makes 8 to 10 servings

Step 5. Removing shell from shrimp.

Step 6. Deveining shrimp.

Step 11. Layering lasagna.

INDEX